SO-AYH-086

Woodward Memorial Library
7 Wolcott Street
Le Roy, New York 14482
DISCARD

- World's Temperate Rain Forests

Things to pack for
rain forest trip:
- Camera and film
- paints, pencils, brush
- sketchbook
- binoculars and
  magnifying glass
- research books
- rain jacket and pants
- waterproof boots,
  hat, and gloves
- umbrella

Yukon
Territory

Alaska

British
Columbia

Canada

United
States

Pacific Ocean

Washington

The rain forest
I visited
(on the Olympic
Peninsula)

Oregon

Canada
United States
North American Rain Forest

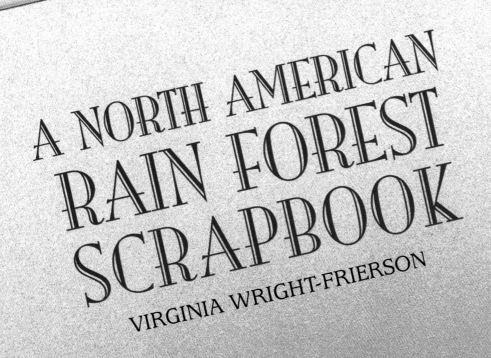

A NORTH AMERICAN RAIN FOREST SCRAPBOOK

VIRGINIA WRIGHT-FRIERSON

Walker and Company
New York

Woodward Memorial Library
7 Wolcott Street
Le Roy, New York 14482

For our family and friends in the Northwest,
especially Michael Daniels, a world-class
teacher and guide!
And with thanks to my sister, Kathleen Tibone,
and her son, Vincent, for exploring this
wonderful forest with me.
Thanks to my husband and children for
sharing it all, and to Soyung Pak, an editor
with vision, enthusiasm, and faith.
— YW-F

Text and illustration copyright © 1999 by Virginia Wright-Frierson

All rights reserved. No part of this book may be reproduced or transmitted in any form or by any
means, electronic or mechanical, including photocopying, recording, or by any information storage
and retrieval system, without permission in writing from the Publisher.

First published in the United States of America in 1999 by Walker Publishing Company, Inc.

Published simultaneously in Canada by Fitzhenry and Whiteside, Markham, Ontario L3R 4T8

The publisher and author would like to thank Janis Burger, park ranger,
Olympic National Park, for her expert advice on this book.

For information about the exploration and preservation of this fragile ecosystem, contact: National
Park Service, Olympic National Park, 600 East Park Avenue, Port Angeles, WA 98362-6798

Library of Congress Cataloging-in-Publication Data
Wright-Frierson, Virginia.
A North American rain forest scrapbook/Virginia Wright-Frierson.
p. cm.
Summary: Presented in the form of a scrapbook, describes the author's exploration
of a temperate rain forest in the continental United States, located in Washington State,
and the plants and animals she found there.
ISBN 0-8027-8679-0 (hardcover). —ISBN 0-8027-8680-4 (reinforced)
1. Rain forest ecology–Washington (State)—Olympic Peninsula—Juvenile literature.
2. Rain forests—Washington (State)—Olympic Peninsula—Juvenile literature.
[1. Rain forest ecology—Washington (State) 2. Rain forests—Washington (State)
3. Ecology. 4. Scrapbooks.] I. Title
QH105.W2W75 1999
577.34'09797'94—dc21   98-42402
                                                                                      CIP
                                                                                       AC

Book design by Rosanne Kakos-Main

Printed in Hong Kong

2 4 6 8 10 9 7 5 3 1

I'm too excited on the plane to read any more about the North American rain forest. So I look at the changing views below me and think and sketch all the way across the continent.

The Atlantic coast of my North Carolina home

The glowing colors of the Appalachians

Quilt patches of midwestern farmland

Brown, barren hills and desert plains

Rocky Mountain peaks and a winding river

Rain forest clouds and the Pacific coast

I am going to Washington's Olympic Peninsula to create a scrapbook about the temperate rain forest. I've been planning this trip for months. But nothing has quite prepared me for the moment when I finally step into this ancient forest. . . .

My eyes must adjust to the bright shafts of sunlight
that shoot through the treetops. In the shadows,
I begin to see every shade of green imaginable.
    The roots of a giant fallen trunk tower over my head
as I set off down the trail to begin my exploration.

The temperate rain forest is sometimes called the ancient, virgin, old-growth, primeval, cathedral, and Sitka spruce forest.

I walk deeper into the forest, listening to the gentle drip of water from the leaf tips, breathing the clean, fresh air that smells like Christmas trees. Then I gaze up . . . and up . . . until I am dizzy. Everything is hushed and quiet. I look around me, half expecting to see elves in this ancient fairyland or dinosaurs from prehistoric times.

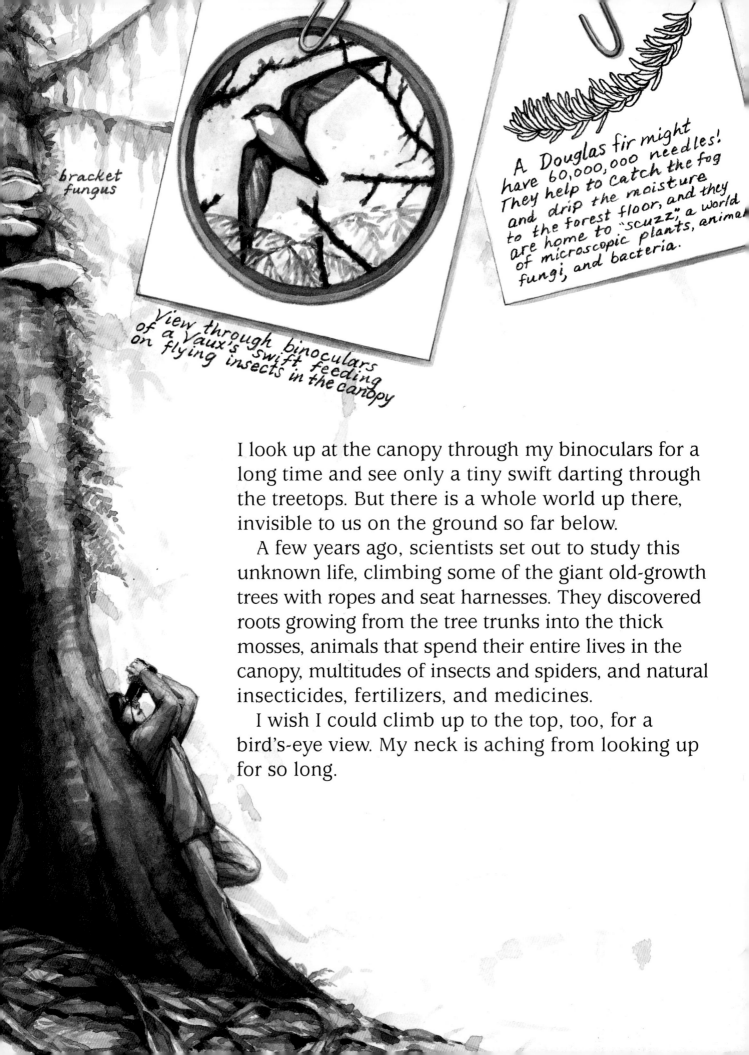

bracket
fungus

A Douglas fir might
have 60,000,000 needles!
They help to catch the fog
and drip the moisture
to the forest floor, and they
are home to "scuzz," a world
of microscopic plants, animal
fungi, and bacteria.

View through binoculars
of a Vaux's swift feeding
on flying insects in the canopy

I look up at the canopy through my binoculars for a long time and see only a tiny swift darting through the treetops. But there is a whole world up there, invisible to us on the ground so far below.

A few years ago, scientists set out to study this unknown life, climbing some of the giant old-growth trees with ropes and seat harnesses. They discovered roots growing from the tree trunks into the thick mosses, animals that spend their entire lives in the canopy, multitudes of insects and spiders, and natural insecticides, fertilizers, and medicines.

I wish I could climb up to the top, too, for a bird's-eye view. My neck is aching from looking up for so long.

I look up "Animals of the Old-growth Canopy"
in my guidebook.

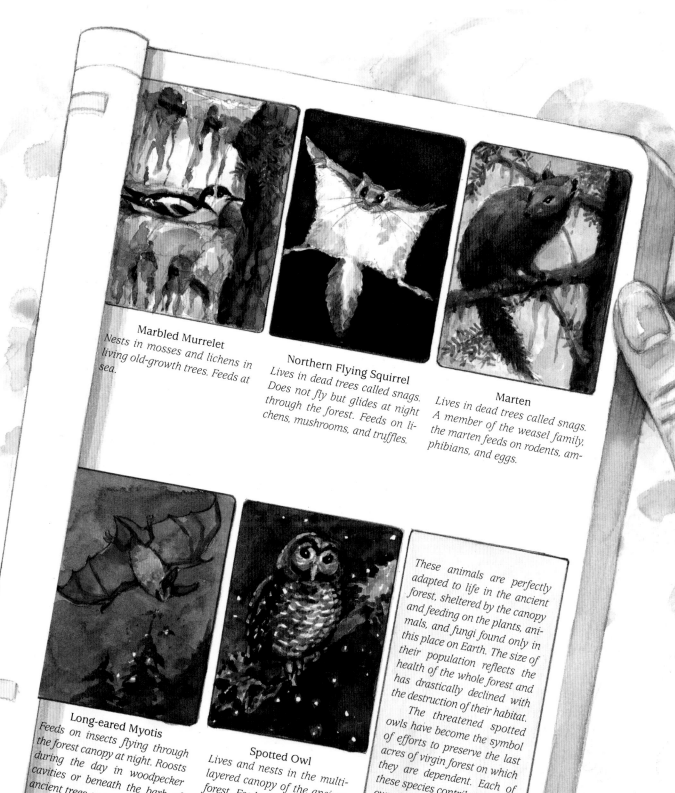

Marbled Murrelet
Nests in mosses and lichens in living old-growth trees. Feeds at sea.

Northern Flying Squirrel
Lives in dead trees called snags. Does not fly but glides at night through the forest. Feeds on lichens, mushrooms, and truffles.

Marten
Lives in dead trees called snags. A member of the weasel family, the marten feeds on rodents, amphibians, and eggs.

Long-eared Myotis
Feeds on insects flying through the forest canopy at night. Roosts during the day in woodpecker cavities or beneath the bark of ancient trees or snags.

Spotted Owl
Lives and nests in the multi-layered canopy of the ancient forest. Feeds at night on small mammals such as mice, voles, woodrats, and flying squirrels, hunting over a large territory.

These animals are perfectly adapted to life in the ancient forest, sheltered by the canopy and feeding on the plants, animals, and fungi found only in this place on Earth. The size of their population reflects the health of the whole forest and has drastically declined with the destruction of their habitat.
The threatened spotted owls have become the symbol of efforts to preserve the last acres of virgin forest on which they are dependent. Each of these species contributes in its own way to the balance of the ancient forest. If one becomes extinct, the whole is threatened.

Pileated woodpecker

I lie down on the mossy ground on thousands of years of decaying wood, leaves, and needles and gaze up at a "snag," a dead tree that is still standing tall. Its bark has sloughed off, and it is full of holes.

A woodpecker hammers in the stillness.

A fallen snag is now a natural bridge.

This giant snag snapped like a toothpick during a windstorm.

Sitka spruce seedlings on a nurse log

Someday the snag will fall and crush everything below. But it will nurture new life as it decays, providing food, moisture, and shelter for animal life and new plant growth. Raised above the crowded forest floor, a fallen trunk is an ideal place for tree seeds to sprout. It may become a "nurse log" supporting a new generation of rain forest trees!

This snag provides a hunting perch and lofty nest for an osprey.

"Fairyland" Rain Forest
Plant Names
Fairybells
Pixie goblets
Enchanter's nightshade
Dragon cladonia
Devil's matchstick
Witch's hair
Gnome-plant
and my favorite...
Fairy barf

My eyes need a rest from looking up this high, so I roll over for a close-up view of the forest floor. Through the magnifying glass I study this miniature meadow.

Rain Forest Plants with
"Food" Names

Candy flower
Skunk cabbage
Salmonberry
Lettuce lung
Licorice fern
Vanilla leaf
Miner's lettuce

"Weird-Sounding" Rain Forest
Plant Names

Laundered rag
Freckle-pelt
Youth-on-age
Inside-out flower
Electrified cat's-tail moss
Toad rush
Pimpled kidney
Lungwort

On a fallen branch, I see tiny mushrooms,
little red-capped lichen (algae and fungi)
called "British soldiers," a baby Sitka spruce,
and . . .

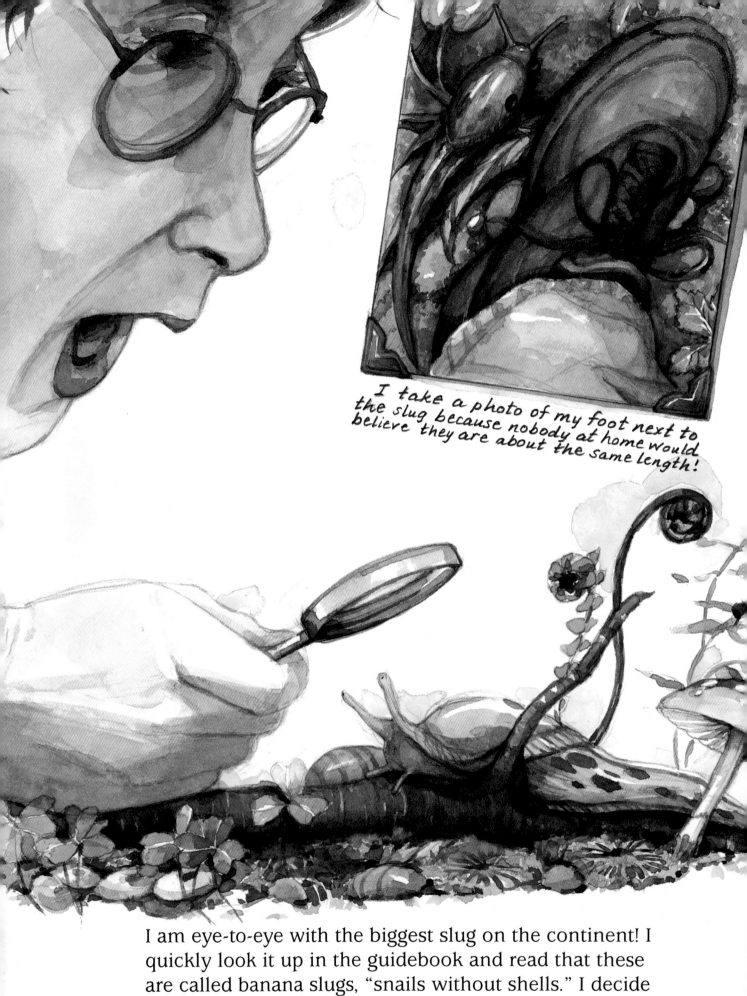

I take a photo of my foot next to the slug because nobody at home would believe they are about the same length!

I am eye-to-eye with the biggest slug on the continent! I quickly look it up in the guidebook and read that these are called banana slugs, "snails without shells." I decide not to lie on the ground anymore.

Douglas squirrel, or chickaree

A Douglas squirrel chatters loudly to let me know I am in its territory. It soon goes back to eating its cone and scattering a few seeds as I quietly take photos and do a quick sketch.

I follow the trail for a long time and see nurse logs
in all their different stages.

Hundreds of seedlings
growing on this nurse log
race to send roots down
to the soil. Only a few
might survive to adulthood.

The trees grow in a straight
line along the nurse log.
This is called a colonnade.

I saw a photo of a totem
pole from a deserted Indian
village. It had fallen over
and become a nurse log as
new life arose on the carved
red cedar.

The nurse log beneath this colonnade has completely rotted away leaving the giant trees standing up on stilts.

I wonder what it would be like to curl up in one of these secret rooms to write and paint and listen and observe. Would I turn green and moldy in a few weeks, covered with moss like the trees?

For thousands of years, American Indians have lived in harmony with the sea and forest on the Olympic Peninsula. From the giant red cedars they made canoes, longhouses, nets, baskets, clothing, tools, and totems.

When European explorers came, they brought metal tools that the native tribes soon began to use for hunting and carving. The explorers also brought diseases that eventually wiped out as much as 90 percent of the native populations. Today, descendants live on coastal reservations: the Makah, Quileute, Hoh, and Quinault.

The Olympic Mountains

This majestic range blocks the clouds and fog rolling in from the Pacific Ocean, creating a rain forest on the western side and almost desert on the "rain shadow," or downwind side, of the range.

Mt. Olympus may receive 200 inches of rain and snow a year, while nearby Sequim receives 17 inches a year.

Hi D. M. + Amy!
I'm sitting on a log in the Hoh river looking at a view of these mountains. It's gorgeous and sunny - not a typical day in the rain forest!
I wish you were with me. You would love it here — Love, Mom

P.S.
I hope to see an elk before I leave

PRINTED IN U.S.A.

Olympic National Park

The trail leads to a sunnier clearing, and I hear the rush of a river and a strange clopping sound. I climb out on a large fallen trunk and listen, peering into the light milky blue of the glacial meltwater. It is the sound of round stones being tumbled along the river bottom by the swift current.

Wright Frierson

I eat my lunch, paint a watercolor of the sparkling
river, and write a postcard, listening, sniffing the
fresh air, and dangling my feet in the icy water. I wish
I had time to follow the river all the way up to the
Olympic Mountains. Maybe I could see an eagle, or
an elk, or a salmon! I begin to walk along the sandy
bank, camera in hand, and step right on a bear track!
I make a U-turn, grab my gear, and race back to the
forest trail.

I head straight for the National Park Visitor Center, where I meet with Mike, the center's naturalist, and several other visitors. He tells us that there can be black bears at the river, especially this time of year when the salmon are running. (Bears love salmon!) He offers to show us a creek where salmon are spawning, and he answers our many questions on the trip.

Q. What is the difference between a tropical and a temperate rain forest?

A. Tropical rain forests are warm all year round and can have almost 35 feet of rainfall a year. There are more species of plants and animals.

Temperate rain forests are cooler in winter and drier in summer, with up to 17 feet of rain a year. While there are fewer different species here, there is more living biomass in the temperate rain forest than anywhere on Earth. And the North American forest is the largest temperate rain forest in the world.

Q. What are the major trees here?

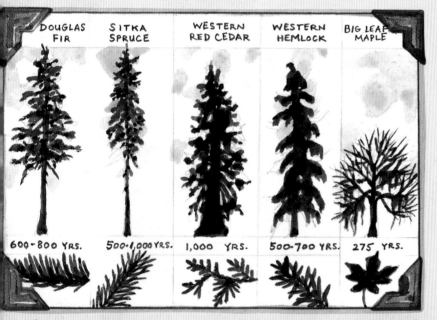

DOUGLAS FIR	SITKA SPRUCE	WESTERN RED CEDAR	WESTERN HEMLOCK	BIG LEAF MAPLE
600-800 YRS.	500-1,000 YRS.	1,000 YRS.	500-700 YRS.	275 YRS.

Q. What are the low-growing trees that are covered with hanging moss?

A. Vine maples. Their branches sometimes root and form arches. Leaves are bright red in the fall.

Mike took a photo of us at the world's largest Sitka spruce: 191 feet tall, 58 feet around, and about 1,000 years old! It is found in the Quinault forest.

Q. Have you ever touched a banana slug?

A. Once I licked one! I was dared by some of the other park naturalists, so I took a good long lick. It left my mouth numb for an hour and it tasted terrible! That is their only defense... don't try it!

We walk down along the creek and see the salmon struggling to swim against the current. I can't believe how exhausted and battered they look. Mike tells us that this is the same stream where these salmon were hatched! As fry, or baby salmon, they fed on insect larvae in the freshwater pools, then swam downstream to the salty Pacific Ocean where they migrated along the coast, eating fish and plankton for a few years.

There, some were eaten by orcas and sea lions, others were caught in fishing nets. Those that survived swam back upstream to the creek where their lives began, to lay thousands of eggs. Soon their amazing life cycle will be over, and they will become food for eagles, bears, seagulls, ravens, otters, and raccoons. I notice an odd branch sticking out of the water and reach to pull it out. Later Mike tells me I have found an antler, shed by an elk in

As the others walk farther along the creek, I stop and sit to write down some of the naturalist's stories before I forget, and to sketch some of the forest patterns I've seen today.

Douglas fir

Western hemlock

Sitka spruce

Western red cedar

Fern frond

Oxalis in the sun

Oxalis in the shade

Wet bird tracks on river stones

Water strider and shadow

Spiderweb after rain

Piggy-back plant

skunk cabbage

Puffballs

Old-growth logs
at a sawmill

Maple wings

Old-man's beard

Salmonberry

Devil's matchstick

Pacific yew

A variety of rain forest mushrooms

Spotted owl
spots

Tailed frog

Skin of a Cope's
Giant salamander

Northern
blue

Fern
stalk

Calypso
orchid

Frost on bigleaf
maple leaves

Fiddlehead

Salal

Horsetail

2 inches

Tailed frogs can be found in the cold, rushing streams and damp forests of the Olympic Peninsula.

Some underground burrowers:

mice + woodrats

shrew moles

red-backed voles

spiders, ants, beetles, termites, centipedes

Townsend chipmunks

earthworms

Many forest animals eat mushrooms and truffles, an underground fungus. They excrete the spores, helping to spread fungi along the forest floor. Fungi help the tree roots to absorb moisture + nutrients.

Walking back, Mike tells us about the underground life of the forest. He lifts up a rotting branch and we find a Van Dyke's salamander and her eggs. We restore its hiding place and hurry on toward the Park Center as the late afternoon sun slants through the trees. Suddenly, we see something I'll never forget . . .

A bull elk stands in the road ahead, his rack of antlers held high. We watch as a herd of thirty or more appears out of the thick, darkening forest, crossing to the river. Then with a snapping of twigs on the mossy ground, the herd moves out of sight.

We have remained frozen except to take pictures. What a perfect way to end the day with my new friends! I promise that someday I'll send them a rain forest scrapbook containing my paintings of them.

Elk create clearings in the forest by browsing on seedlings. In study areas that have been fenced to keep elk out, the understory quickly grows into a tangled thicket, too dense to walk through.

Years ago, it became fashionable for men to wear an elk canine tooth on their gold pocket watches. To meet the demand for elk teeth, the herds were hunted almost to extinction (much like the killing of elephants just for their ivory tusks). Now they are protected, and their numbers are stable in the Olympic National Park.

What We Can Do to Help Preserve Our Forests

Walk carefully and quietly in the forest
Stay on trails
Don't litter
Pick up trash left by others
Don't smoke
Put out campfires
Don't waste paper
Don't use paper or Styrofoam cups
    or plates
Recycle glass, cans, and paper
Use cloth towels, diapers, and
    napkins instead of paper

I drive slowly out of the National Park, hoping to see the sunset over the Pacific Ocean a few miles away. Soon I pass acres and acres of clear-cut forest lands, whole mountainsides shaved bare. Trucks loaded with logs roar by. I drive past a modern sawmill and see thousands of logs in piles; some are old-growth giants waiting to be sawed into lumber, shingles, and plywood. The smell of sawdust is in the air.

Rows of replanted trees

Logging has long been a part of this peninsula, where trees grow quickly in the abundant rainfall and rich soil.

Tree seedlings must be replanted within a few years of clear-cutting. The new forest is again ready for harvest in a few decades, all the trees the same age and size. Only the virgin forest has new and ancient trees growing together, snags, decaying fallen trunks, a many-layered canopy, and the rich underground life that all work together in delicate balance.

• In 1938, the Olympic National Park was named.
• In 1976, it was designated a Biosphere Reserve by the United Nations.
• In 1981, the Olympic National Park was also designated a World Heritage Site.

Though new logging methods are being tried and preservation efforts are continuing, only a small percent of the ancient forest remains, and old-growth trees are still being cut.

I drive to a ridge and walk among the giant knotted cedar trees until the dark canopy suddenly opens to endless sky and ocean. I want to remember this golden light for the last pages of my rain forest scrapbook. For a long time I look over the rocky sea stacks and countless logs that have drifted down rivers or fallen from the cliffs to wash up in piles on the shore like giant bleached bones.

I stand alone under the trees that were here hundreds of years before Columbus sailed to America, listening to the eternal waves and watching as the same stars appear.

CAUTION !

BANANA SLUG CROSSING

WH
watchi

AMI HAZA

IN CASE OF EARTHQU
HIGH GROUND OR

TIMBER
MUSEUM
FORKS.wash

E
577.3409   16.85
WRI

Wright-Frierson
  A North American rain forest scrapbook

WOODWARD MEMORIAL LIBRARY
7 Wolcott Street
Le Roy, NY 14482

Please return materials promptly.
Fines are charged for overdues.
Borrowers will be held responsible
for loss or damage to materials.

DISCARD

577.3409   WOODWARD MEMORIAL LIBRARY
WRI

A North American rain forest

0061998